www.finishinglinepress.com

Hunger Anthem

poems by

Joseph Helminski

Finishing Line Press
Georgetown, Kentucky

Hunger Anthem

Publisher: Leah Huete de Maines
Editor: Christen Kincaid
Cover Art: Joseph Helminski
Author Photos: Jane Ahern

Order online: www.finishinglinepress.com
also available on amazon.com

Author inquiries and mail orders:
Finishing Line Press
PO Box 1626
Georgetown, Kentucky 40324
USA

Table of Contents

My Fellow Americans 1

Mission Accomplished.. 2

Lingua Franca 3

Formerly Known As.. 4

Pest Control.. 5

Climate Science... 6

Bible Lesson... 7

Spring and Summer Almanac.. 8

Binge Watch Aesthetics... 9

Carpe Diem 10

Old School.. 11

Under Siege 12

Expiation.. 13

Observed.. 14

The Evidence 16

Blanc... 17

Fingers of the Hand... 18

Art School... 19

Commerce 20

Walt Whitman 21

Self-Reliance.. 22

Blood Moon 23

Mnemosyne... 24

Breath.. 25

This book is dedicated to Jane.
I owe you poems other than these.

My Fellow Americans

Sweet land of libertines, you who
feed on news streams,
self-care manuals,
coffee, roll-ups,
opiates,
punch,
encapsulated fecal matter to restore withered gut flora,
oil, electricity,
the poor,
their children,
the old, their assets,
emojis,
data storage, clouds and pixels,
would you please pass over my house?

I have smeared my patriot lintel
with the blood of strange labor,
a clear sign that I only
allow delivery from fulfillment services.

That anointing stuff comes in vials
from a warehouse states away,
and in my dreams
I wash down goodies from free buffets
with rushing, glugging red,
iron taste reaching
like love of country down, down,
down, and
deep.

Mission Accomplished

Bailing out and circling the bilge drain,
we shouldn't mind if the charts get wet.
After all, not a page shows how to keep afloat
after we poked holes in everything
to peep through a latticed world.
Now that we've satisfied our curiosity
in query after query,
we can see to the bottom of the ocean
and beyond to the molten core,
its colors an unsettling beauty that
(our mistake!) was not for us.
Although we don't have enough aircraft,
winging it looks like a last option
until our arms get heavy enough
to cross over our chests as the undead do
waiting for the night to fall.

Lingua Franca

To ask what happened to old expressions
("Take a long walk off a short pier,"
"There's one born every minute")
that finally died out on contact with an ear
is to answer your own question.
New versions arrange themselves
like ancient ideograms, now scrollable,
virtual, customizable, unlike Uncle
who chuckled for the hundredth time
at "Just don't call me late for supper."
We have lots to choose from
among all those user-friendly scripts.
Even the ancients knew that
giving the people what they want
is something for everyone.

Formerly Known As

Recall the consuming world,
dynamo of headlong leapers?

Hazardous telephone cords stretched
across halls in private consults,
knives scraped marrow,
and no one read the manual.

Chemistry brought quality
to rain, and the children's overalls
were stuffed with rocks.

Where sharp plastic appeared
in a bun or a jug,
it was wondered at.

Horoscopes scrutinized
the future as a gleaming sedan
pulled up to the door
of our next house.

And when it thundered,
it thundered so hard
the lightning
stopped coming out.

Pest Control

Mouse, snatched from the cat's mouth,
twitches outdoors where you tossed it.

You set traps around the foundation, seal holes.

One morning two and the next three
make ways in like stubborn facts.

The woods are full of them,
heard from the deck as rustling leaves.

You can always burn them out,
douse and torch the undergrowth.

A barn owl shrieks at the updraft.

Climate Science

One scheme would revive the mammoth
to graze the taiga and arrest earth's thaw
where methane bubbles below
threatening our last undoing.
It's a conceivable triumph,
staggering tons of flesh and bone, a gene-spliced Jesus.
Elsewhere families move toward borders
once carved cleanly as fruit
from storied orchards.

Bible Lesson

Sound the sirens.
Throw down your pots and pans,
dig your new hole in the ground.
Men once wore signs to say the end is near.
They thought of fires, not coasts
awash in melting ice,
never knowing the angels
want to drown us in our own talents
for taking parables too much to heart.

Spring and Summer Almanac

Hinges dropped from doors.
Birds sang to insomnia.

Nuts showered yards
in the driest month to date.

News forced eyes on the drowned,
their mouths agape.

Prairie fires roared,
tribal boundaries burning.

Saturday's monthly siren
mocked all our preparations.

Former freewheeling pleasure anthems
claimed you as white noise.

Binge Watch Aesthetics

The sound air makes escaping the mouth
just after a fist hits the gut
could be art for the right audience.
The hissing of spray canisters
might be a glissando
to accompany the cries of the vanquished.
Underneath, boots keep the beat,
armies merging onto bodies,
collapsing lungs and piercing
hopes on spear tips.
Teasing overtures promising
evil and virtue
engaged in mutual torture
tell you this will be a good episode.

Carpe Diem

Dawn
Floral rows bow
at their green waists
as you walk to the garage,
and it's about time, you think,
and back over them.

Afternoon
Breathing onions and gum after lunch,
you write the required self-assessment,
and in the nap that follows
wrestle an angel
who displaces your hip effortlessly.

Evening
Clean glass forgotten,
you walk through the door wall
and do not pick up the shards.
You beat the appliances and cook beans
over burning tires in the yard.

Night
By streetlight
a riderless horse lurches
under saddlebags
bulging with unread books,
not for sale.

Sleep
Nothing in the dictionary
suggests the word counterpane
has any resemblance
to its own sound,
but you still fall under
your own body's spell.

Old School

Remember bruises and shiners, fat lips and iodine?
How we could hardly wait for the lunch bell
to squeeze the Jell-O,
rub it into brushed hair,
squirt milk through a nostril,
slap around the sandwiches?
Remember the wet towels?
The pats and grins?
We were kings of the mountain,
shoving losers into corners,
told not to act that way
because whatever.
We made it, played hard, worked harder.
We own the debt to show it,
and we won't be blamed,
and honey, we're home.

Under Siege

Who knew wet nails
could make so much noise
scratching glass?

Rain's diffuse body
seems to want in.
You don't blame it
but won't let it.

Anyway, there's too much.

One drop, and soon
the whole floor
is promiscuous leakage,
causing you trip and lose
the position gained
after walking in the front door
so many years ago.

Maybe rain should be bolder,
but its lot is to be rain,
and glass is glass,
and stone is stone,
and borders borders,
and just in case,
you seal your palace
with evaporating fire,
self-sacrifice
hoses will call heroism.

Expiation

I dreamed what it would be like
to be a soldier in an army marauding,
watched rebel heads swing like naked bulbs
over the bar where foreign correspondents buzzed
filing reports on the conditions
as I set to getting drunk and threw rocks
over the stray dog fields
under the guise of victim.

Observed

I.
In the desert gas is scarce,
but if you run out
you can try patience,
the most worthless virtue.

II.
The manager wants to know
if everything is delicious
and carries a blackjack.

III.
Civility's heart is to avoid offense,
which could mean nothing doing
or cardiac arrest.

IV.
Whoever called it Old Spice
must have had a funny story about
choosing the name
and what was once called fun
by certain winking men.
Nobody laughs driving a Ram,
pinched by Under Armour, half-blind in Oakleys.

V.
Celebrating your day
in the blank card section
so I can rechristen
your fortune in terms I will
conjure at home
and sprinkle from a lachrymatory.

VI.
Hip injury
would not have fazed Jacob
had he had a CPL.

VII.
Take this brick and eat of it
so that you will not rise.

VIII.
Words have less power than we know.
Take powder keg,
which only sounds like
a place for makeup applied
before a show that killed.

IX.
So many people want fairness but know
only cruelty and lack
that I feel sorry for those performing the ceaseless work
of undoing, and the constant need
to find ways to clean up all that blood
without touching it.

The Evidence

Although I agree with many theorized critiques of capitalism, I still like to open the refrigerator and find brand labels meeting me at eye level. Sometimes I even open the door to turn jars and containers at the right angles to please my sight when I go for a snack or a seltzer. Part of me recognizes the possibility that this habit may have been formed by the insidious and mercenary workings of advertising over a lifetime, but I think it has more to do with well-balanced and thus delightful arrangements of color and shape. I think of what it would be like if the shelves contained only homemade foods and leftovers in wrinkled lumps of plastic. Worse still is opening the freezer to find vacuum sealed bags labeled in permanent marker like the detritus collected from a crime scene and placed in an evidence locker in a room at the back of a police station where the word "individual" is used in place of "person" in reports composed across from a squat public building or a boarded up grocery that closed 10 years ago when the Wal-Mart came to town with its automatic doors and its greeter and its neatly arranged stacks and shelves where the labels always face out.

Blanc

If we're turning the page, we can't
write history without it.
The script can't contain everything.
It must begin somewhere, have a middle and an end.

In the common metaphor, what does not belong
is self-duplicating cancer, cancelling
out the good by overcrowding.
Increase and multiply got us so far.
It's time to to stable the stock, bar the door.

We can write all that: a making, a growing,
a gathering, a keeping.
The problem is the ink and its color
to cut, leaving all untold.

Fingers of the Hand

I have tried to befriend you,
shake hands, which means my fist relaxes.

What sort of handshake
is the first problem.
Different styles send messages,
so I let your hand take charge
and we get over that.

What is left to say?

That I am not regretful?
That no one in my history
as far as I know contributed
to this situation?
That I'm sad it exists,
as when I read bad news?

We are together, after all,
in this feed,
getting run over, being displaced,
shooting, getting shot,
although some are luckier than others.
History, an accident
I had no say over,
put me on this side of the tracks,
but we can press the flesh until the next train
arrives to take you wherever it's going
as I wave goodbye, which won't be forever,
living as we do under my roof
in what my hands did not build
where we awaken in the same bed,
strangers in the same house.

Art School

While our country drove to work,
we learned to make pointless efficiencies:
red rubber balls to spill from the carry-on
at the feet of the TSA;
fishing lures in the medicine cabinet,
train of hooked lies;
gray skulls overhanging the haciendas;
twisted paper,
an ouroboros.
Meanwhile, file drawers jam and screens freeze.
So much gets undone in the work of doing.
In another chamber, patriots chortle over historic bones.
Now the familiar seasons come to their close.

Commerce

The day will come for that glittering occasion,
you in a suit of fine linen, quaffing red wine,
fearless of stain or accident.
You will be the idol of that present
in that suit before an admiring audience
that has worked so hard to recognize you.

Even if not, you have chances left.
Formal wear is frequently on sale.
You could also head in the direction
of sandals, anorak and stick,
humble and unbranded.
You could make something precise, not cordial,
to be found in decades
by a distant curious family member
or sensitive estate sale shopper.

At present is just the sense
that time has been sent to your location,
that you've torn the strip from its container
and are thus out of any right to be unfulfilled.

Even if you're alone,
it's a good bet someone expects
you're just thumbs-a-twiddle, lid heavy,
thinking about your next meal
or how tomorrow will bring a surprise
or how the next minute will flash you.

On your mind's distant shore, you have taken up an art
in a stone house on a silent coast.
The water is a blue without a name.
No one knows you.
Your canvases, strange and bold,
are heaved to the sea and hold the wind.

Walt Whitman

Our boots are caked in blood.
You said you would stop somewhere, waiting.
I imagined your arms widening to take us all in
after we rounded what we swore
was the last blind corner.
I had faith that you were the landscape,
the same I walked,
not an abstract of the spirit
but that thing, the corn in the sun.
When I was a pilgrim crossing
the lake prairies on a train
I fed on your catalogs.
Each word pointed to itself,
to every other declaiming
we are all each other.
Such a loving trick.
Where do you wait for us?

Self-Reliance

If my own body is not me, but Nature,
what right do I have to pick at it?

Then again, I cannot just observe it
as I do the grass beyond the window
or the deer that eat the hostas
and strip bark from the pear tree,
innocent acts of survival and presence.

My body means to hurt me,
springing blisters and wringing its nerves (are those not me?)
over the slightest insult or over
having to send itself into the world mornings,
me with(in) it.

When it got angry and swept books off the table
I call it a series of accidents,
atomic in origin,
of me, not on me.

Blood Moon

It casts shadows and I remember
a woman who walked near the house
where I stood inside watching her
watching me, child touching glass
above the lot where after snow
my mother stood with me
admiring its clean surface.
Tonight new snow outside my house
is still smooth, and the moon whitens it more,
and I watch it fall as if it were alive,
as if the world were only quiet,
and it falls and deepens,
and I am safe behind the pane
as I watch it fall and deepen.

Mnemosyne

Nameless ghost, lurching forward among meadow flowers,
no scatterings spell your course.
Some say farmers see you in abandoned houses
tilting into homestead plains.
Farmers say migrating flocks have the best views
where they seem to pause their flight,
and I want to ask, who recalls
last season's birds?

Breath

Breath is not a body,
but when it ends
the motions do too,
the skin turns,
and the rest tightens
into a prop yet still
steals the scene.

It is a good actor,
talking to you all that while it lasts
and telling you what the rest wants
if it is bold,
or turning inward
to be held
by the body that stirred it,
fearing any distance from home
and lingering at
an enameled threshold,
after a while
sent out
again and again
one day never returning,
its house undisturbed.

Joseph Helminski was born in Detroit in 1970. He attended the University of Michigan as an undergraduate, and earned his Ph.D. in English at Wayne State University. He has taught at Wayne State, the University of Toledo, and since 2006 has been a full-time faculty member at Oakland Community College in Oakland County, Michigan. He has published work on the lesser-known novels of Harriet Beecher Stowe in *Beyond Uncle Tom's Cabin*, book reviews in *American Literature*, and is a two-time NEH Fellow. He began publishing poetry in 2015. *Hunger Anthem* is his first published book. He lives with his wife, Jane, in Farmington Hills, Michigan.